W9-BTT-415

Learn to Draw

DINOSAURS

www.av2books.com

Go to www.av2books.com, and enter this book's unique code.

BOOK CODE

E996347

AV² by Weigl brings you media enhanced books that support active learning.

AV² provides enriched content that supplements and complements this book. Weigl's AV² books strive to create inspired learning and engage young minds in a total learning experience.

Your AV² Media Enhanced books come alive with...

Audio
Listen to sections of the book read aloud.

Key Words
Study vocabulary, and complete a matching word activity.

Video
Watch informative video clips.

Quizzes
Test your knowledge.

Embedded Weblinks
Gain additional information for research.

Slide Show
View images and captions, and prepare a presentation.

Try This!
Complete activities and hands-on experiments.

... and much, much more!

Published by AV² by Weigl
350 5th Avenue, 59th Floor
New York, NY 10118
Website: www.weigl.com www.av2books.com

Library of Congress Cataloging-in-Publication Data

Dinosaurs / edited by Jordan McGill.
p. cm. -- (Learn to draw)
Includes index.
ISBN 978-1-61690-860-7 (hardcover : alk. paper) -- ISBN 978-1-61690-866-9 (alk. paper) -- ISBN 978-1-61690-990-1 (online)
1. Dinosaurs in art--Juvenile literature. 2. Drawing--Technique--Juvenile literature. I. McGill, Jordan.
NC780.5.D56 2011
743.6--dc23
2011020311

Printed in the United States of America in North Mankato, Minnesota
1 2 3 4 5 6 7 8 9 0 15 14 13 12 11

062011
WEP290411

Project Coordinator: Jordan McGill
Art Director: Terry Paulhus

Every reasonable effort has been made to trace ownership and to obtain permission to reprint copyright material. The publishers would be pleased to have any errors or omissions brought to their attention so that they may be corrected in subsequent printings.

Weigl acknowledges Getty Images as its primary image supplier for this title.

Contents

Why Draw?

Drawing is easier than you think. Look around you. The world is made of shapes and lines. By combining simple shapes and lines, anything can be drawn. An orange is just a circle with a few details added. A flower can be a circle with ovals drawn around it. An ice cream cone can be a triangle topped with a circle. Most anything, no matter how complicated, can be broken down into simple shapes.

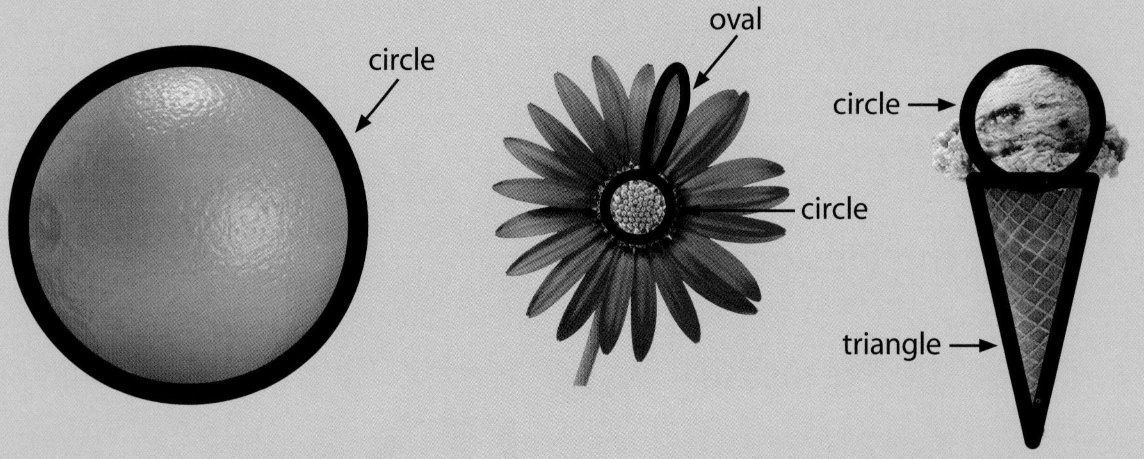

Drawing helps people make sense of the world. It is a way to reduce an object to its simplest form, say our most personal feelings and thoughts, or show others objects from our **imagination**. Drawing an object can help you learn how it fits together and works.

What shapes do you see in this car?

It is fun to put the world onto a page, but it is also a good way to learn. Learning to draw even simple objects introduces the skills needed to fully express oneself visually. Drawing is an excellent form of **communication** and improves people's imagination.

Practice drawing your favorite dinosaurs in this book to learn the basic skills necessary to draw. You can use those skills to create your own drawings.

Dinosaurs

Dinosaurs are fun to draw. It is hard to imagine that these giant creatures existed at one time. As you draw each part of the dinosaurs in this book, consider how that part benefits the creature. Think about how the dinosaur would survive without that feature.

Long before humans lived, dinosaurs roamed Earth. They ruled the world for 150 million years. During this time, some dinosaurs became the biggest and strongest animals ever to walk on land. Dinosaurs became **extinct** 65 million years ago. No other group of large animals has managed to live as long as the dinosaurs.

Meet the Plesiosaur

Plesiosaurs were a group of long-necked water animals that lived from about 215 million to 65 million years ago. Early plesiosaurs, such as the plesiosaurus, were about 15 feet (4.6 meters) long. Later plesiosaurs, such as "Predator X," reached lengths of up to 50 feet (15 meters). A "Predator X" fossil was found in 2009. The animal most likely weighed more than 100,000 pounds (45,359 kilograms).

Flippers
Plesiosaurs swam by flapping their **fins** in water. They swam as if they were flying through the ocean.

Jaw
Plesiosaurs had strong jaws. The jaw of "Predator X" is thought to have produced the strongest bite of any known animal, ever.

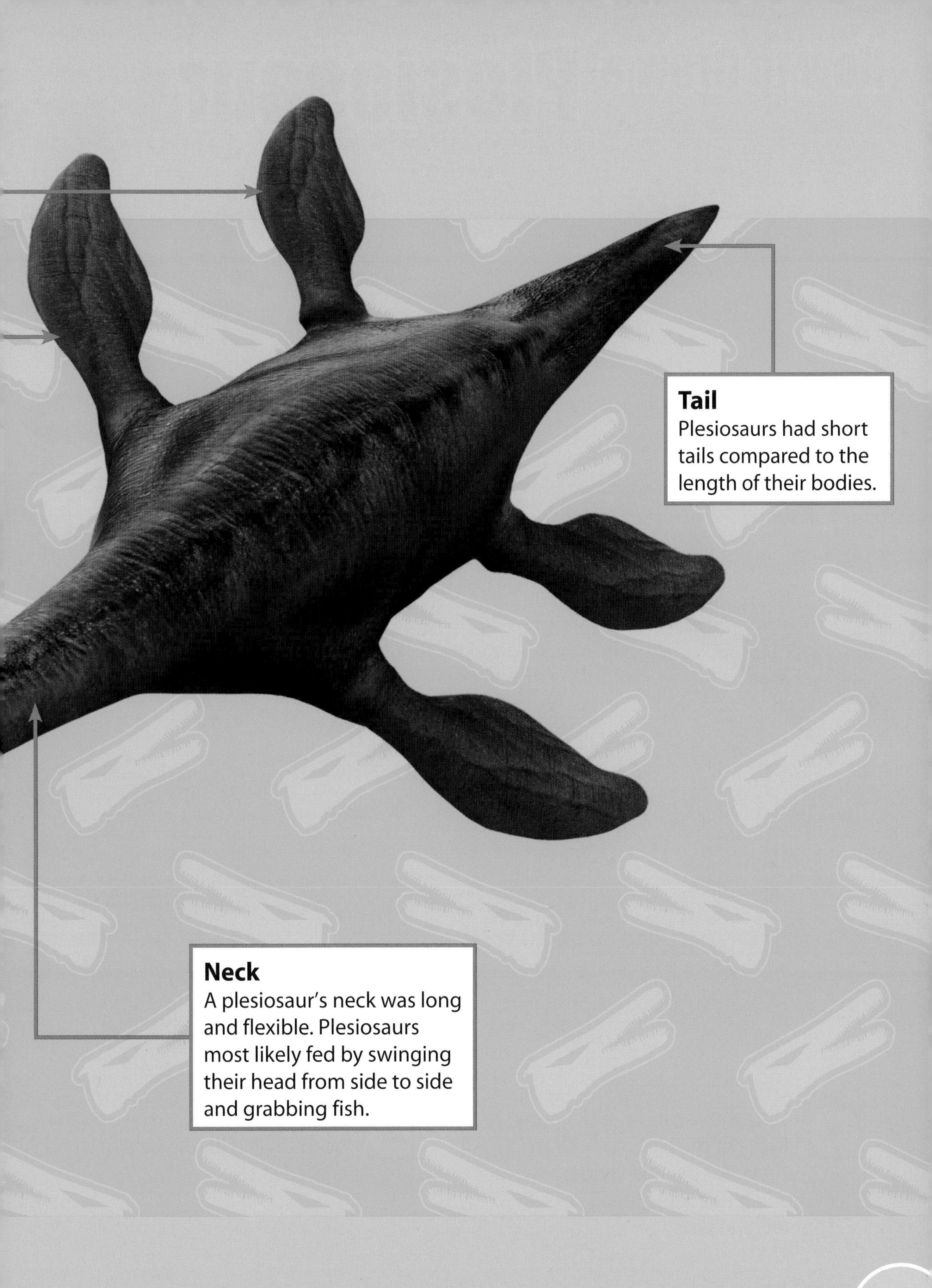
Tail
Plesiosaurs had short tails compared to the length of their bodies.
Neck
A plesiosaur's neck was long and flexible. Plesiosaurs most likely fed by swinging their head from side to side and grabbing fish.

How to Draw a Plesiosaur

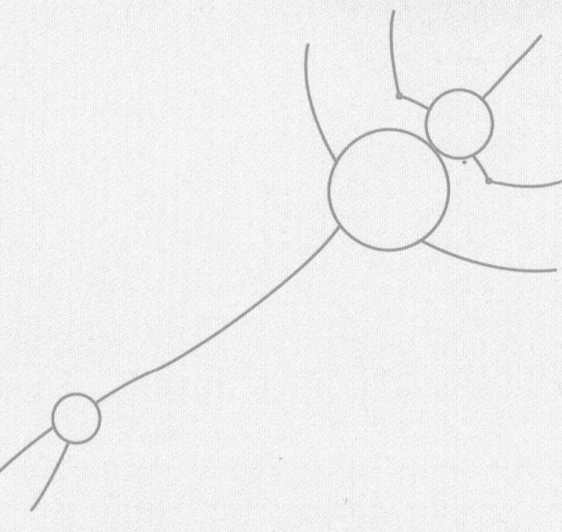

1. Start with a simple stick figure frame of the plesiosaur. Draw circles for the head and body, and lines for the limbs, neck, tail, and jaws.

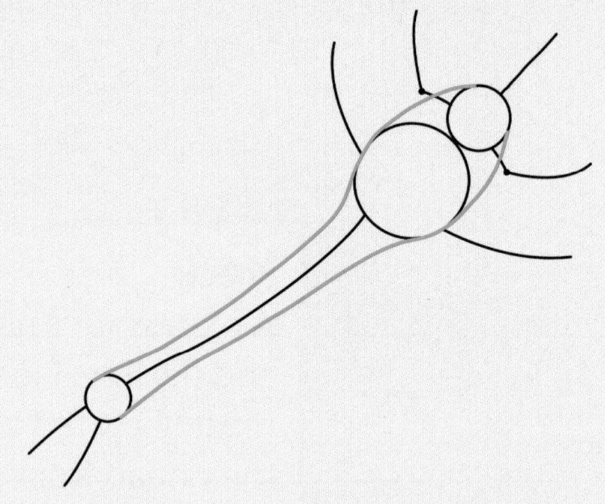

2. Join the two body circles and the head circle with the help of smooth curved lines.

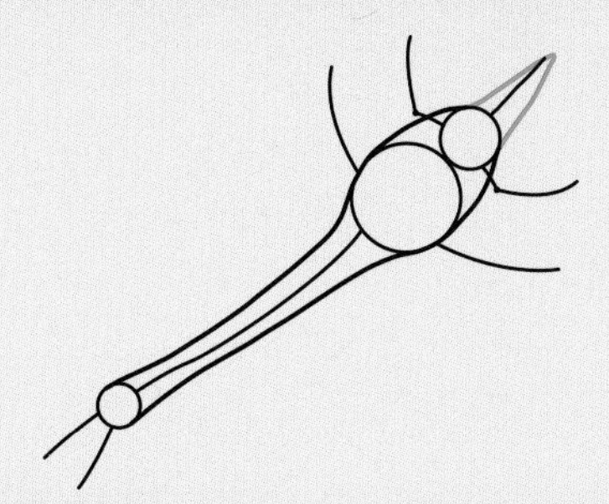

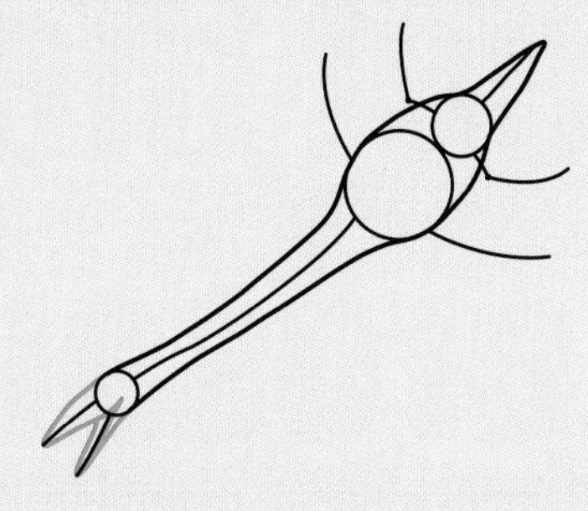

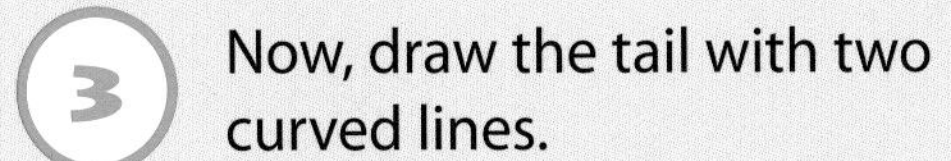

3 Now, draw the tail with two curved lines.

4 Next, draw the jaws by connecting the head circle with jaw lines.

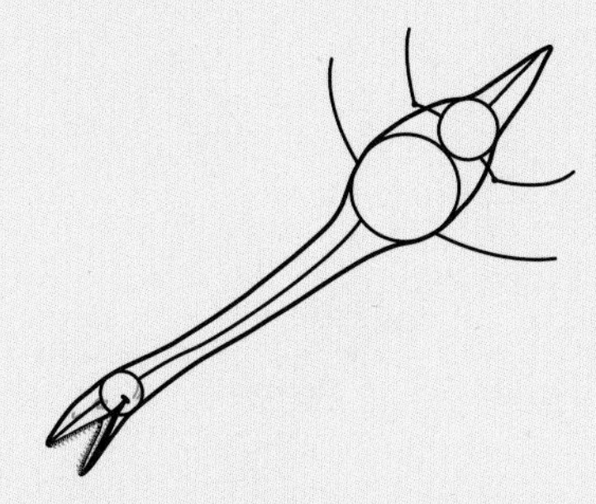

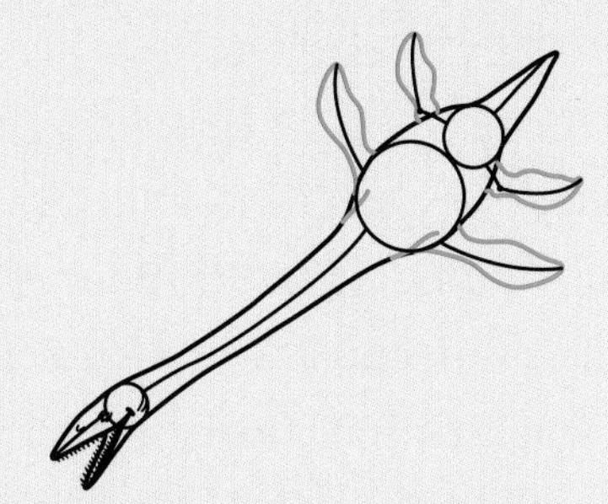

5 In this step, draw the eye, teeth, and nostril. Also, draw curved lines near the mouth.

6 Draw the limbs with curved lines, as shown. These will serve as plesiosaur's flippers.

7 Draw curved lines on the body, head, neck, and limbs.

8 Finally, erase the extra lines and stick figure frame.

9 Color the picture.

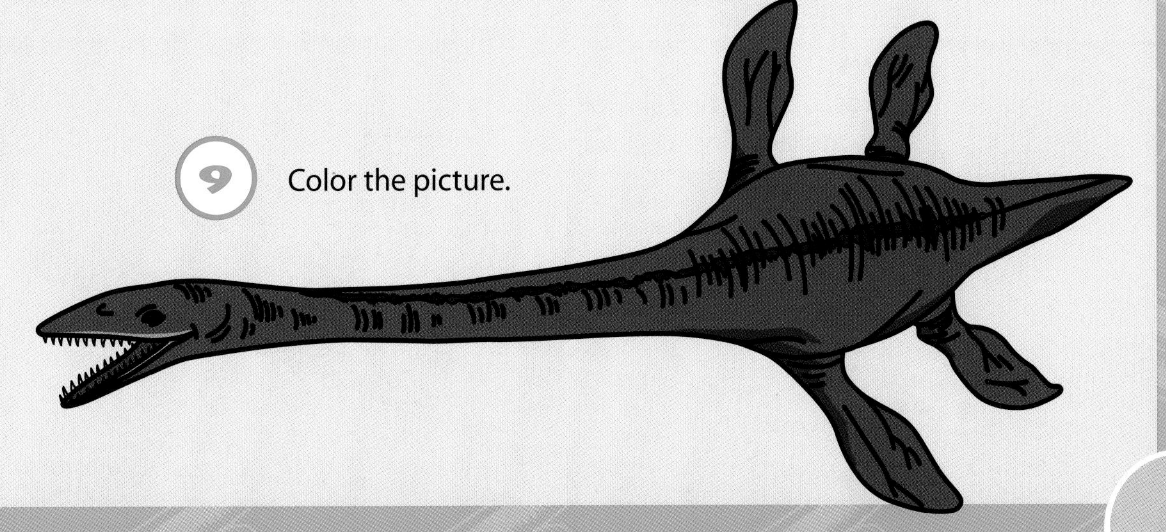

Meet the Pterosaur

Commonly called pterodactyls, pterosaurs are the first creatures with a spine to be able to fly. Researchers think that pterosaurs mostly lived in caves and trees. Pterosaurs were present on Earth for more than 150 million years. They went extinct about 65 million years ago. Most likely, pterosaurs were capable hunters that were able to fly very fast. They could dive from the air and pluck fish from the water.

Bones
Pterosaurs had **hollow** bones, much like birds. This made pterosaurs light enough to fly.

Jaws
Pterosaurs had tiny sharp teeth. They ate large insects and fish.

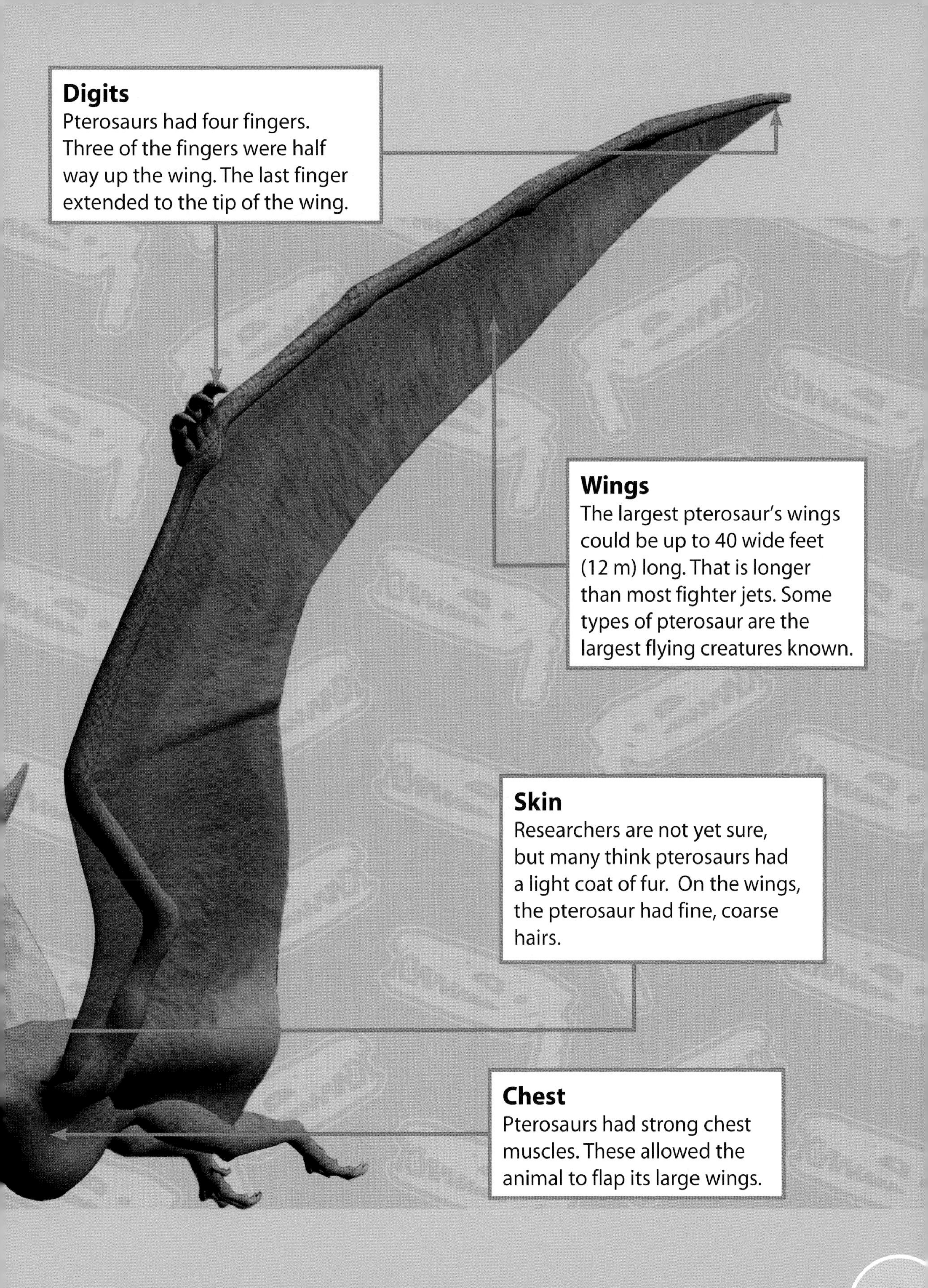
Digits
Pterosaurs had four fingers. Three of the fingers were half way up the wing. The last finger extended to the tip of the wing.
Wings
The largest pterosaur's wings could be up to 40 wide feet (12 m) long. That is longer than most fighter jets. Some types of pterosaur are the largest flying creatures known.
Skin
Researchers are not yet sure, but many think pterosaurs had a light coat of fur. On the wings, the pterosaur had fine, coarse hairs.
Chest
Pterosaurs had strong chest muscles. These allowed the animal to flap its large wings.

How to Draw a Pterosaur

1. First, draw a stick figure frame of the pterosaur. Draw circles for the head and body, and lines for the limbs, neck, wings, beak, and head point.

2. Draw the head crest and join the body circle and head circle with smooth curved lines.

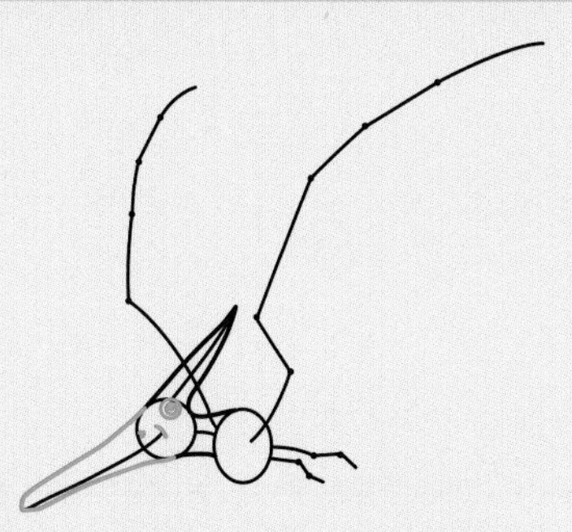

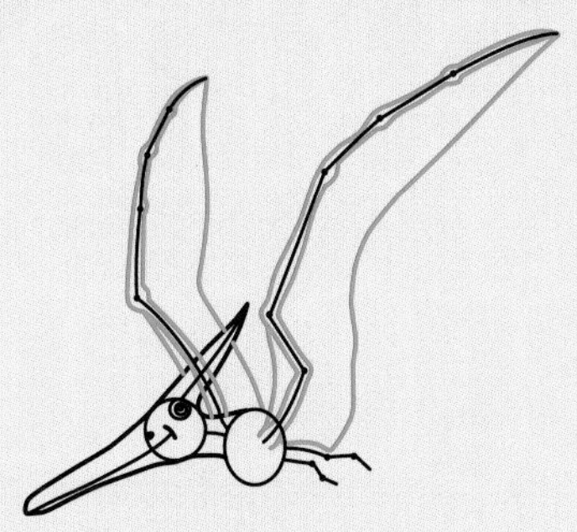

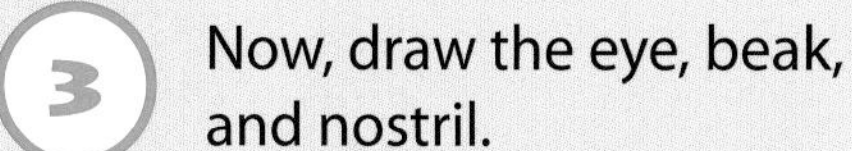

3 Now, draw the eye, beak, and nostril.

4 Next, draw the wings with smooth curved lines.

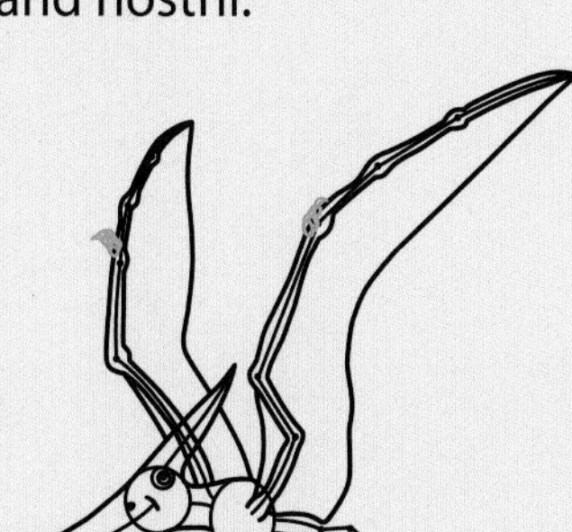

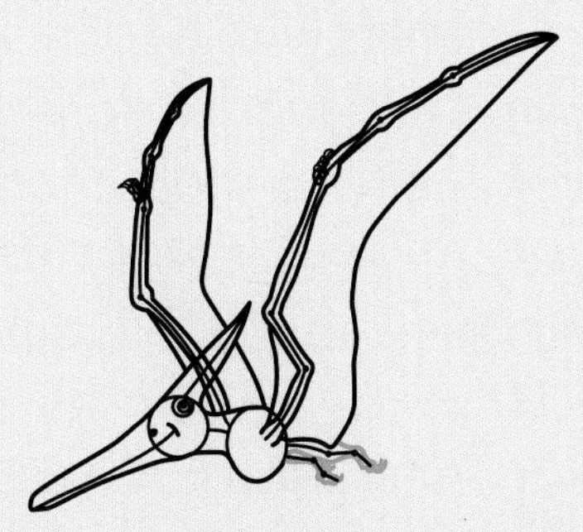

5 In this step, draw the wing digits.

6 Draw the limbs with curved lines, as shown.

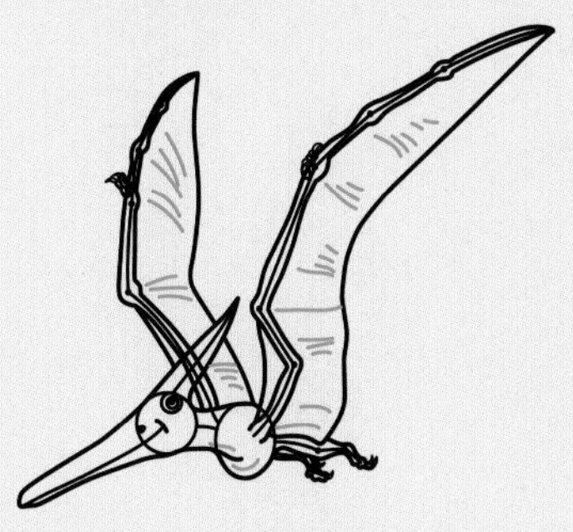

7 Draw curved lines on the body and wings.

8 Erase the extra lines and the stick figure.

9 Color the picture.

Meet the Stegosaurus

Stegosaurus were large four-legged animals with a spiked tail and a line of triangular spikes on their back. Some were more than 30 feet long (9 m) and 14 feet (4 m) tall. Stegosaurus lived about 150 million years ago. Most often, stegosaurus **fossils** are found in North America, though they have been found in Europe as well.

Brain
Stegosaurus had one of the smallest brains of all dinosaurs. Their brain was about the size of a walnut.

Beak
Stegosaurus had no front teeth. Instead, they had a beak. A stegosaurus would eat by pulling plants off trees and swallowing without chewing.

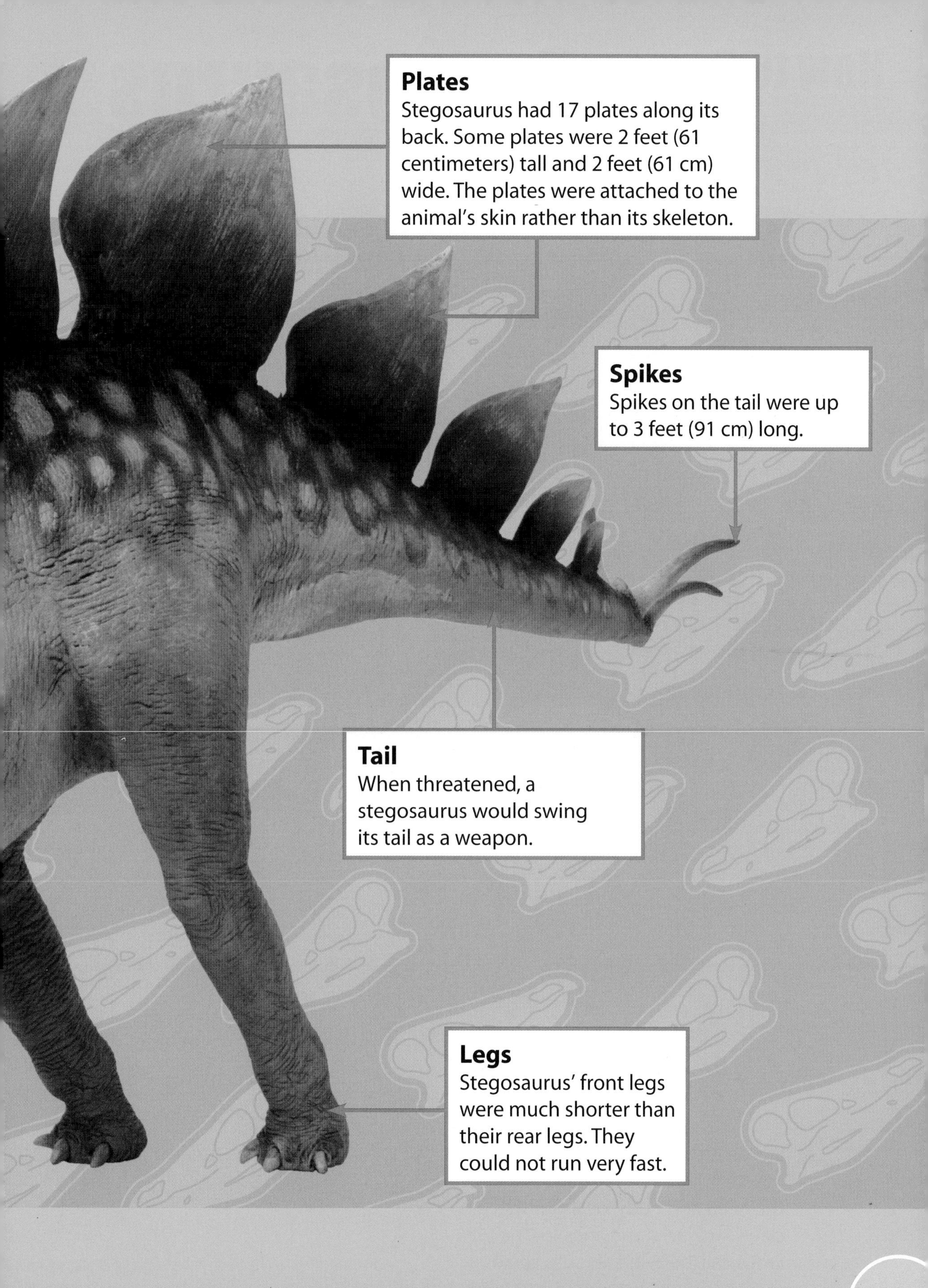
Plates
Stegosaurus had 17 plates along its back. Some plates were 2 feet (61 centimeters) tall and 2 feet (61 cm) wide. The plates were attached to the animal's skin rather than its skeleton.
Spikes
Spikes on the tail were up to 3 feet (91 cm) long.
Tail
When threatened, a stegosaurus would swing its tail as a weapon.
Legs
Stegosaurus' front legs were much shorter than their rear legs. They could not run very fast.

How to Draw a Stegosaurus

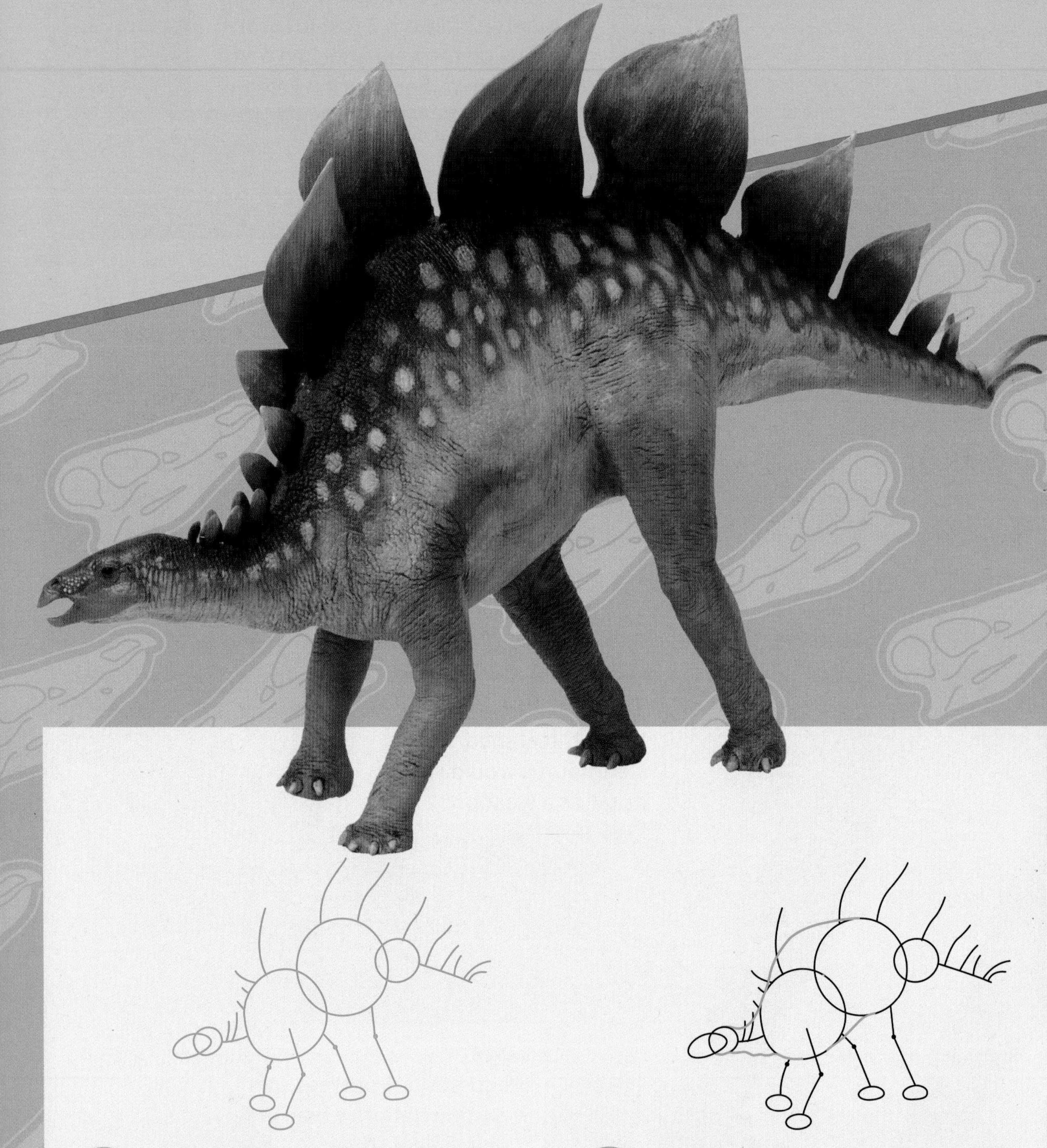

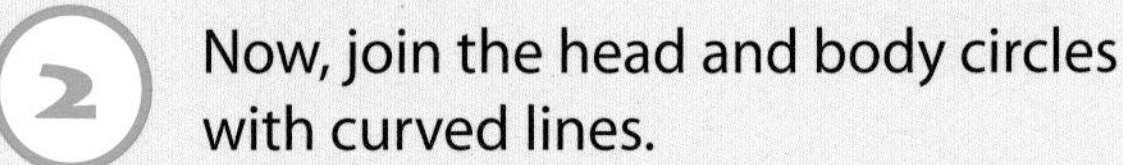

1 Start with a stick figure frame of the stegosaurus. Draw circles for the head and body, ovals for the claws and jaws, and lines for the limbs, tail, body plates, and spikes.

2 Now, join the head and body circles with curved lines.

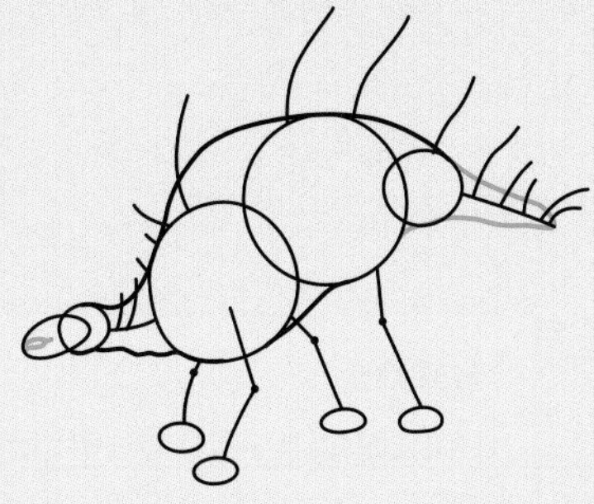

3 Next, draw the mouth and tail, as shown.

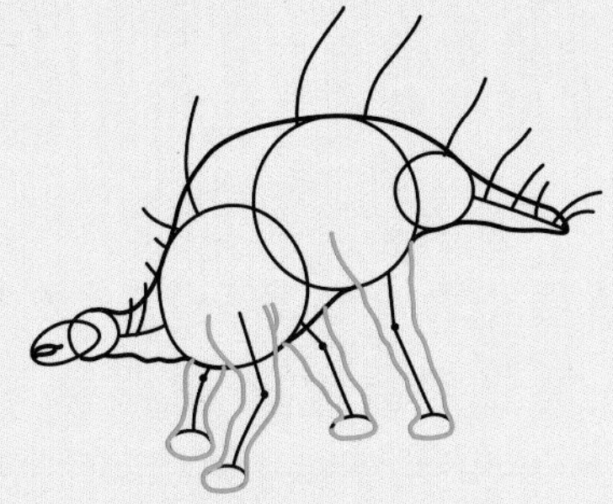

4 In this step, draw the limbs.

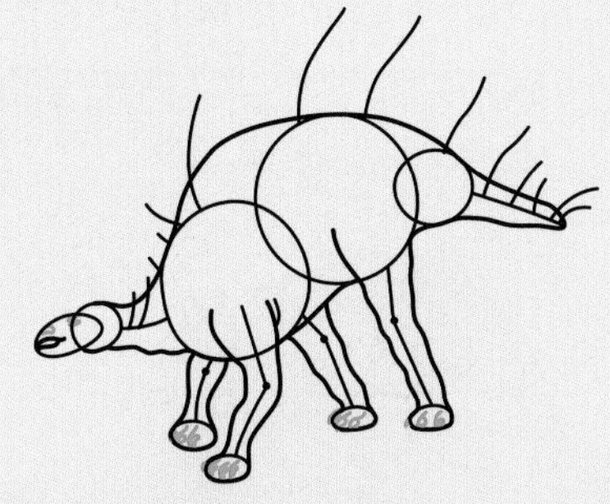

5 Draw the eye, nostril, claws, and nails, as shown.

6 Next, draw the body plates and spikes with curved lines.

7 Draw the body spots with the help of small lines and circles.

8 Erase the extra lines and stick figure frame.

9 Color the picture.

Meet the Triceratops

Triceratops means "three-horned face" in Latin. These dinosaurs were given that name because of their three large horns. Triceratops were up to 30 feet (9 m) long and weighed more than 12,000 pounds (5,443 kg). The last triceratops lived more than 65 million years ago.

Horns
Triceratops had three large horns, one above each eye and another above the nose. Some triceratops had horns more than 3 feet (91 cm) long.

Beak
Triceratops had a beak for clipping plants. Inside, the lower jaw was lined with sharp, shearing teeth. These **adaptations** helped triceratops eat plants.

Bony Frill
The bony frill was solid bone. The frill had many small spikes along its edge.
Feet
A triceratops had three-hoofed front feet and four-hoofed back feet. It could run about 21 miles (34 km) per hour.

How to Draw a Triceratops

1 Start with a stick figure frame of the triceratops. Draw ovals for the head and feet, and circles for the body. Use lines for the limbs, tail, horns, and head frill.

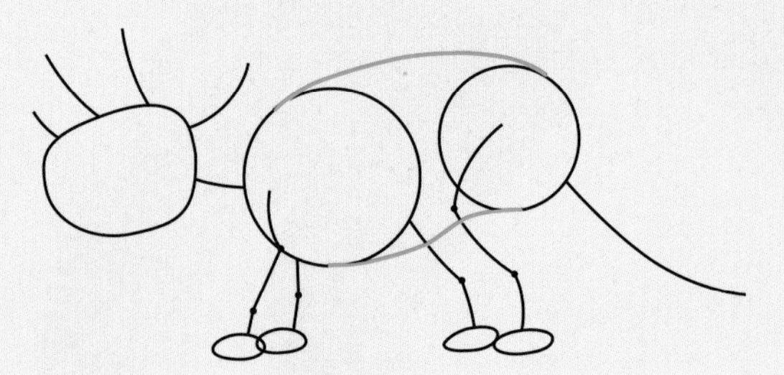

2 Now, join the body circles with curved lines.

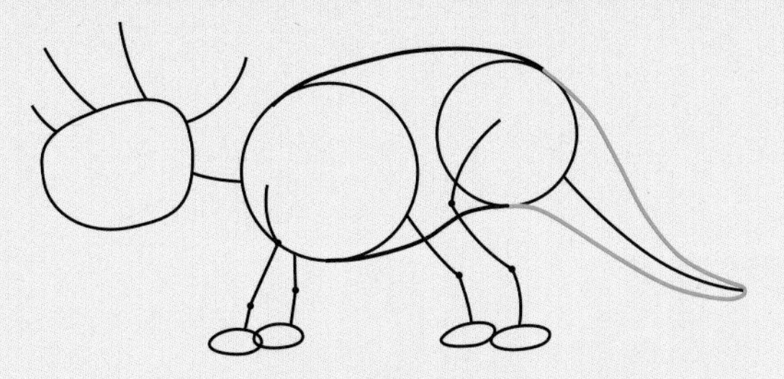

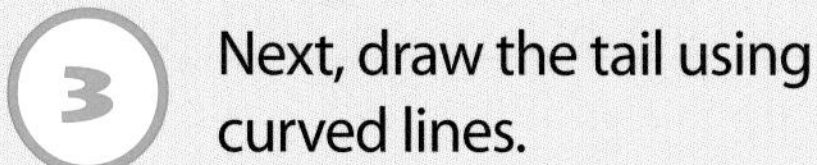

3 Next, draw the tail using curved lines.

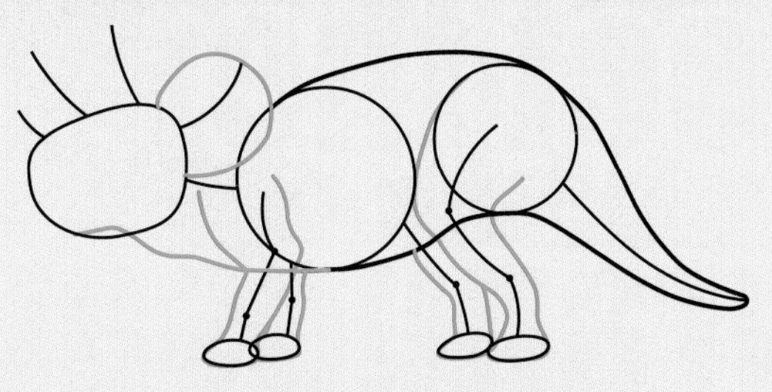

4 In this step, draw the limbs, head frill, and neck using a circle and curved lines.

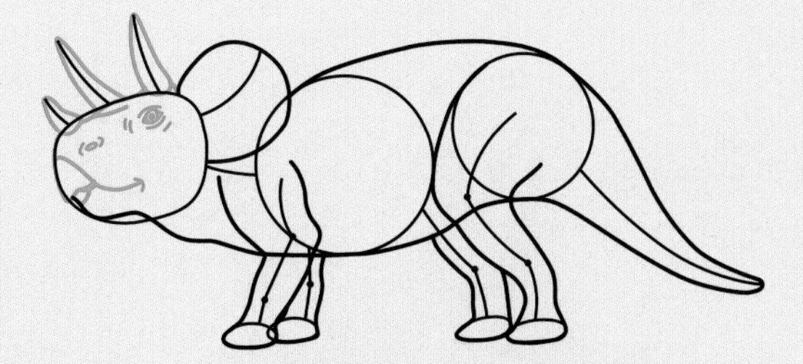

5 Draw the eye, nostril, horns, and mouth.

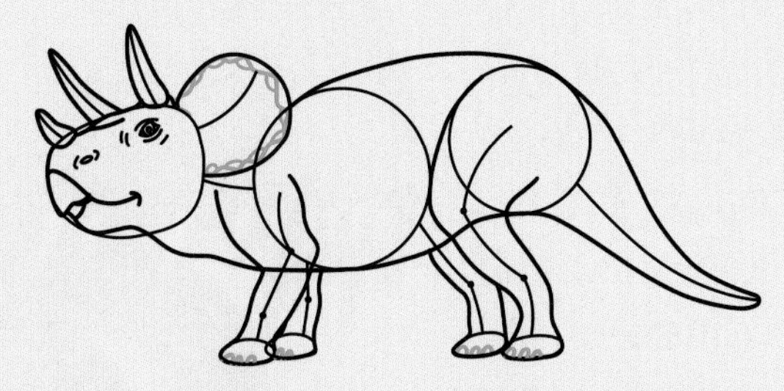

6 Next, draw the frill curves and claws, as shown.

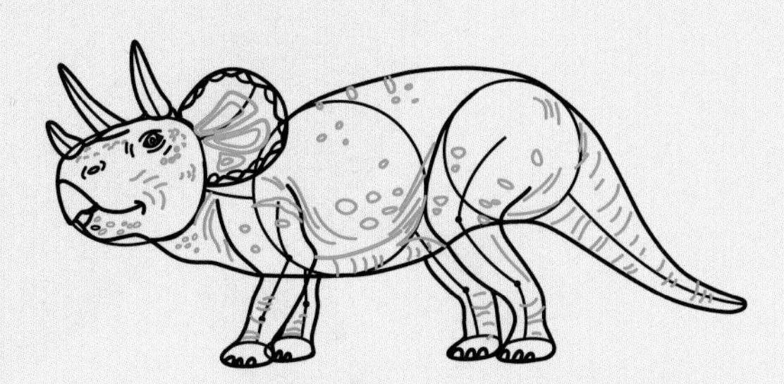

7 Draw curved lines and small circles on the head, body, and limbs. Also, draw triangular shapes on the frill, as shown.

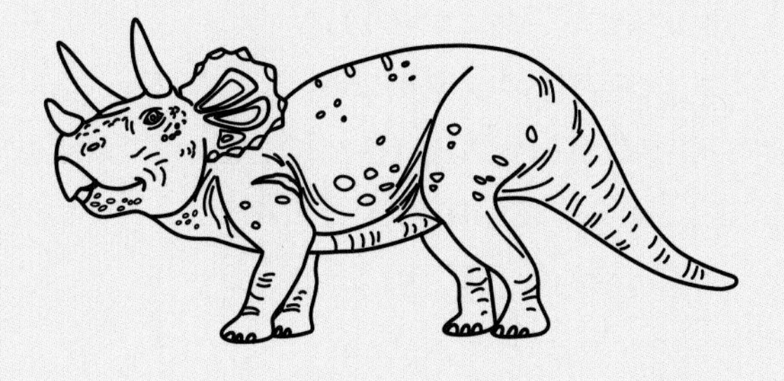

8 Erase the extra lines and stick figure frame.

9 Color the picture.

Meet the Tyrannosaurus Rex

Tyrannosaurus rex, or T. rex, is considered by some to be the king of dinosaurs and is most likely the best-known dinosaur. In Latin, its name means "king of the tyrant lizards." T. rex was more than 45 feet (14 m) long and weighed up to 15,000 pounds (6,800 kg). A T. rex could stand up to 21 feet (6 m) tall. Some scientists think that a T. rex could eat up to 500 pounds (227 kg) of meat in one bite.

Teeth
Inside the large mouth of a T. rex were about 60 teeth that were up to 6 inches (15 cm) long. The bite of a T. rex was very strong. It could tear the roof off a car.

Clawed Fingers
T. rex's arms, each with two fingers at the end, were quite short. They could probably grab and hold prey, but they were too short to pass food to the mouth.

Eyes
A T. rex's eyes allowed it to judge the distance of prey well. This made the T. rex a capable hunter.

Tail
A T. rex had a very heavy head and chest. The long tail helped the T. rex balance when it ran.

Legs
A T. rex had large, strong legs and was able to move quite fast for its size. It could run about 20 miles (32 km) per hour.

How to Draw a Tyrannosaurus Rex

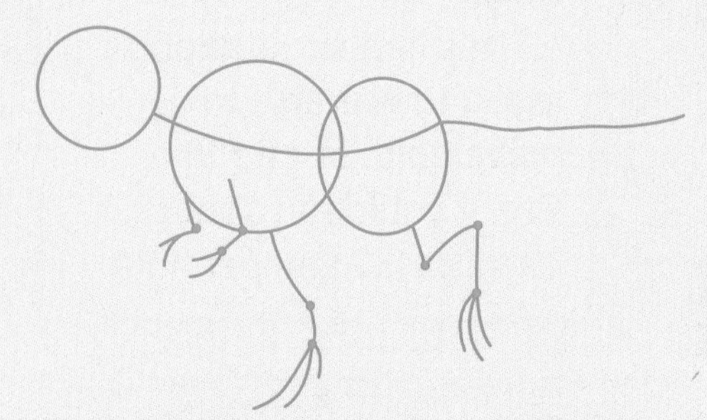

1 Start by drawing a stick figure frame of the Tyrannosaurus rex. Use circles for the head and body and lines for the tail and limbs.

2 Now, join the head and body circles with curved lines, and draw the jaws.

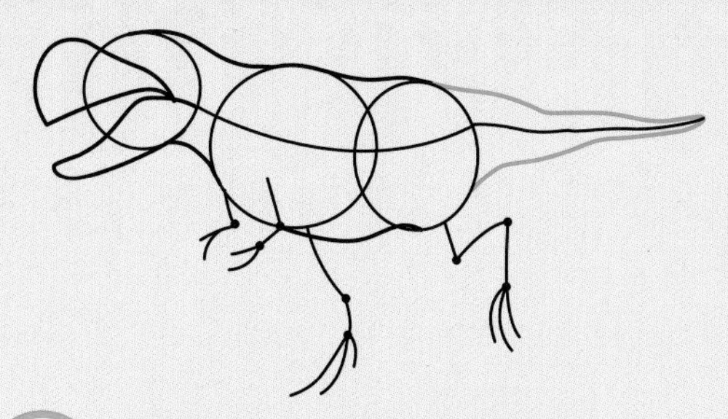

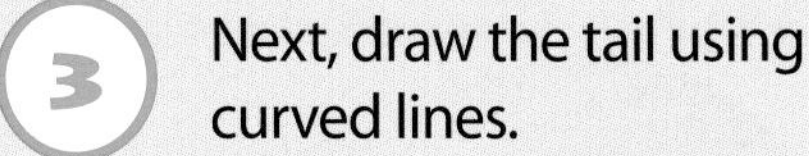

3 Next, draw the tail using curved lines.

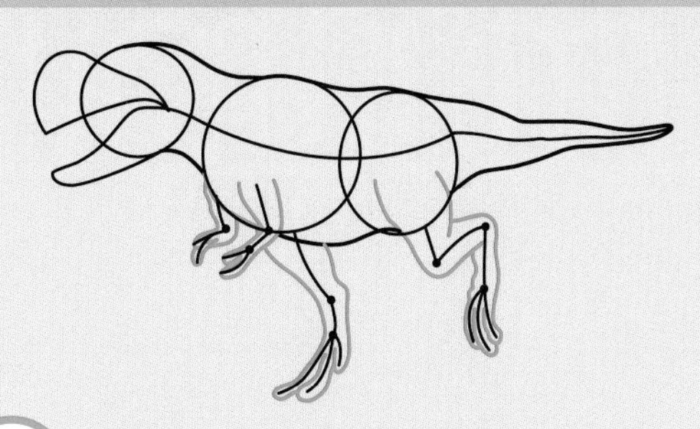

4 In this step, draw the limbs using curved lines.

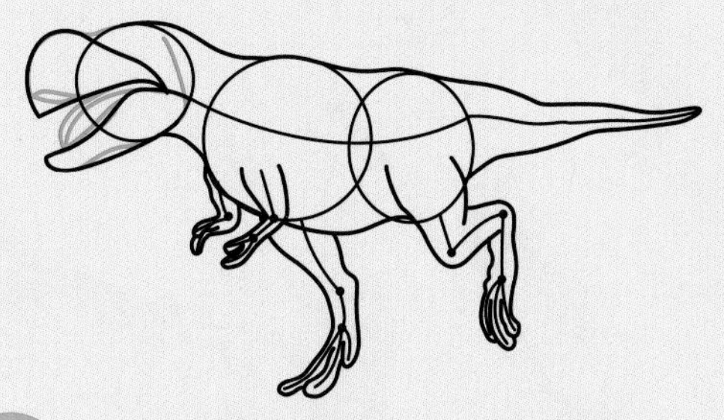

5 Now, complete the jaws by drawing curved lines, as shown.

6 Next, draw the eye, teeth, nostril, and nails, as shown.

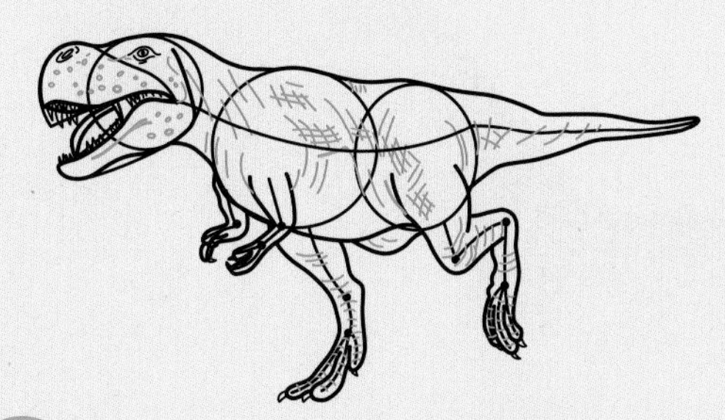

7 Draw small circles on the head, and curved lines on the limbs, body, and tail.

8 Erase the extra lines and stick figure frame.

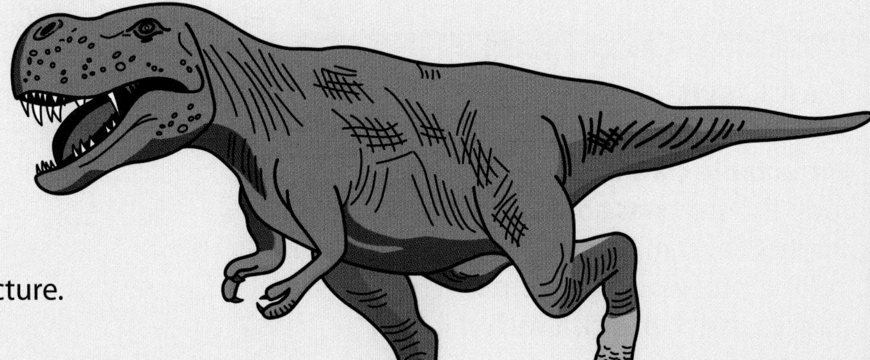

9 Color the picture.

Meet the Velociraptor

Velociraptors were small by dinosaur standards. They were meat eaters that most likely hunted in packs. They also were very smart when compared with other dinosaurs. Velociraptors had large brains for their body size. Most velociraptors were less than 6 feet (1.8 m) tall. Much like birds, velociraptors had hollow bones and laid eggs. They also may have had feathers. Velociraptors most likely last walked Earth more than 65 million years ago.

Teeth
Velociraptors had 80 sharp teeth. Each tooth was up to 1 inch (2.5 cm) long.

Foot Claws
Velociraptors had one long, **retractable claw** on each foot. The claw was about 3.5 inches (9 cm) long. A velociraptor would grab onto its prey and then kick it with its back claws.

Tail

The tail of the velociraptors was made of hard bone. It was not very flexible. The tail was mainly used for balance while running, jumping, and hunting. Velociraptors may have balanced on their hard tail and sliced other animals with their sharp foot claws.

Legs

Powerful legs and its low body weight allowed the velociraptor to run up to 24 miles (39 km) per hour.

How to Draw a Velociraptor

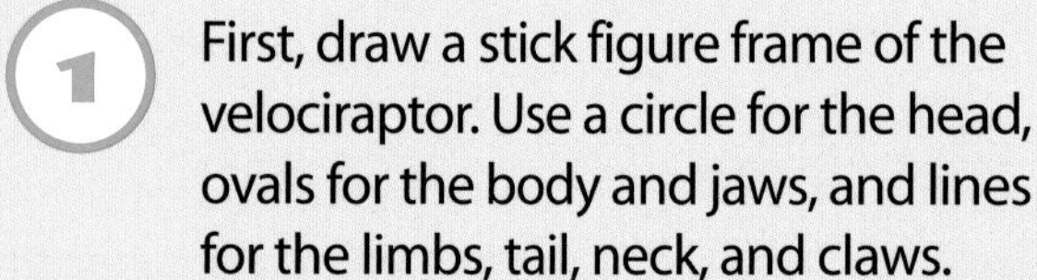

1. First, draw a stick figure frame of the velociraptor. Use a circle for the head, ovals for the body and jaws, and lines for the limbs, tail, neck, and claws.

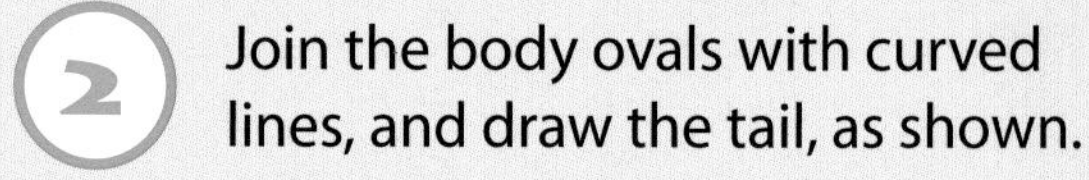

2. Join the body ovals with curved lines, and draw the tail, as shown.

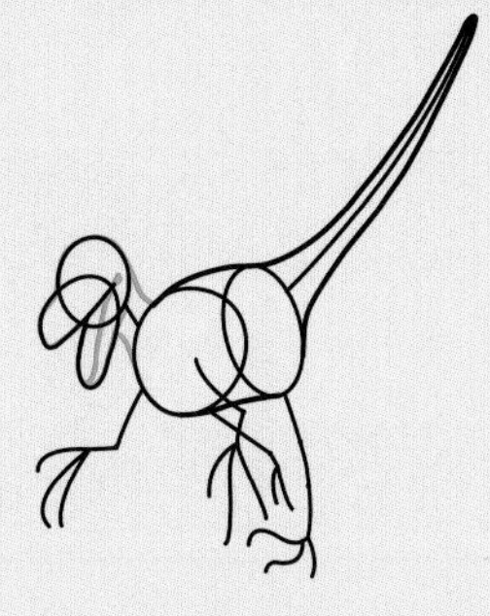
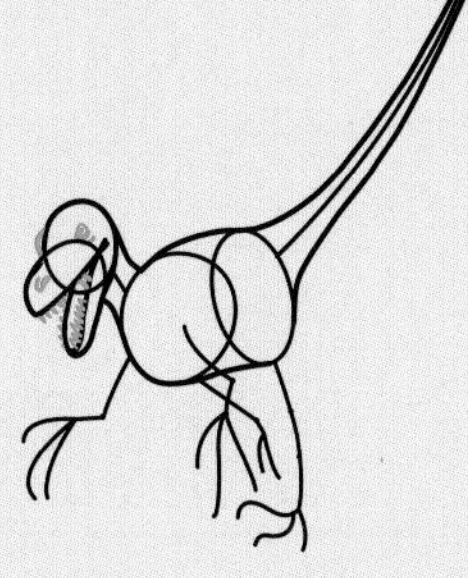

3 Now, draw the neck and jaws using curved lines.

4 Next, draw the eyes, teeth, and nostril, as shown.

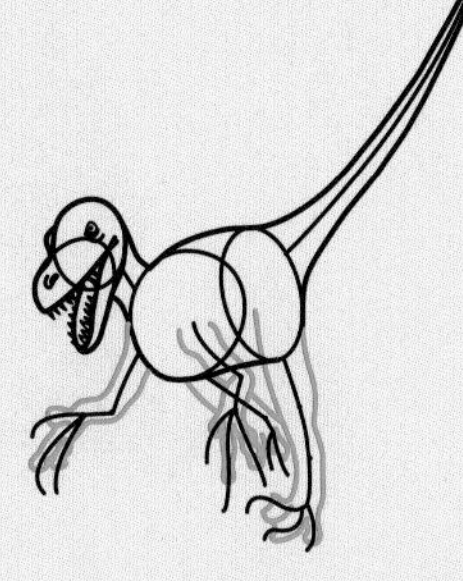

5 In this step, draw the arms and legs, as shown.

6 Draw the nails with curved lines.

7 Draw curved lines on the body, head, tail, and limbs. Also, draw small circles on the head.

8 Erase the extra lines and the stick figure frame

9 Color the picture.

Test Your Knowledge of Dinosaurs

1\.

The jaw of what animal is thought to have produced the strongest bite ever?

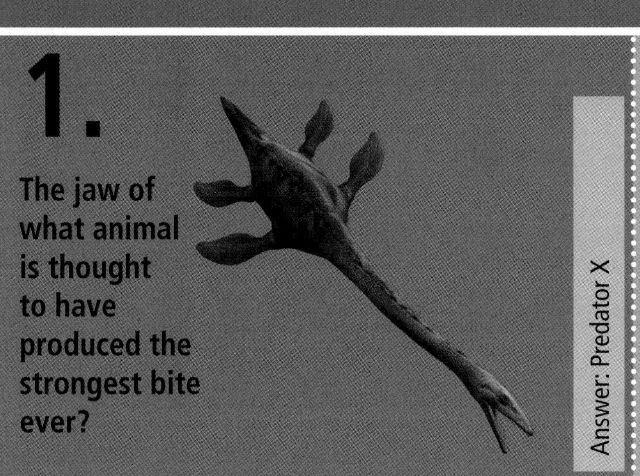

Answer: Predator X

2\.

The largest pterosaur's wings could be how wide?

Answer: 40 wide (12 m) wide

3\.

How long ago did the stegosaurus live?

Answer: About 150 million years ago

4\.

How long could a triceratops horns grow?

Answer: More than 3 feet (91 cm) long

5\.

Tyrannosaurus rex means what?

Answer: King of the tyrant lizards

6\.

How tall were most velociraptors?

Answer: Under 6 feet (1.8 m) tall

Want to learn more? Log on to av2books.com to access more content.

Draw an Environment

Materials

- Large white poster board
- Internet connection or library
- Pencils and crayons or markers
- Glue or tape

Steps

1. Complete one of the dinosaur drawings in this book. Cut out the dinosaur.
2. Using this book, the internet, and a library, find out about your dinosaur and the environment in which it lives.
3. Think about what the dinosaur might see and hear in its environment. What does its environment look like? What sorts of trees are there? Is there water? What does the landscape look like? Are there other dinosaurs in its environment? What in the dinosaur's environment is essential to its survival? What other important features might you find in the dinosaur's environment?
4. On the large white poster board, draw an environment for your animal. Be sure to place all the features you noted in step 3.
5. Place the cutout dinosaur in its environment with glue or tape. Color the animal's environment to complete the activity.

Glossary

adaptations: adjustments to different conditions or environments

communication: the sending and receiving of information

extinct: no longer alive anywhere on Earth

fins: a flat part of a water animal used to steer and balance

fossils: the rocklike remains of ancient animals and plants

hollow: empty inside

imagination: the ability to form new creative ideas or images

retractable claw: a claw that can be pulled back into the paw when not in use

Log on to www.av2books.com

AV² by Weigl brings you media enhanced books that support active learning. Go to www.av2books.com, and enter the special code found on page 2 of this book. You will gain access to enriched and enhanced content that supplements and complements this book. Content includes video, audio, web links, quizzes, a slide show, and activities.

Audio
Listen to sections of the book read aloud.

Video
Watch informative video clips.

Embedded Weblinks
Gain additional information for research.

Try This!
Complete activities and hands-on experiments.

WHAT'S ONLINE?

 Try This!	 Embedded Weblinks	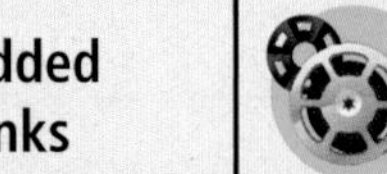 Video	EXTRA FEATURES
Complete an interactive drawing tutorial for each of the six dinosaurs in the book.	Learn more about each of the six dinosaurs in the book.	Watch a video about dinosaurs.	**Audio** Listen to sections of the book read aloud.  **Key Words** Study vocabulary, and complete a matching word activity.  **Slide Show** View images and captions, and prepare a presentation.   **Quizzes** Test your knowledge.

AV² was built to bridge the gap between print and digital. We encourage you to tell us what you like and what you want to see in the future.

Sign up to be an AV² Ambassador at www.av2books.com/ambassador.